The Secret

By Jacqueline Robinson

Published by Jewelmark Press 2016

Copyright © 2016 Jacqueline Robinson

A CIP record for this book is available from the British Library

ISBN 978-0-9562727-2-0

Cover Design by Michelle Broughton

I dedicate this book to, Nyamekeyi, Asore and Viola

Other Books by
Jacqueline Robinson

Silence is Broken

Passages

A voice from behind the veil

Forward

The Secret is the title poem for this anthology which describes the stigma sometimes faced by families living with mental illness. The poem looks at how the very act of maintaining a secret can be soul destroying. Other poems in this collection draw our focus to situations faced on a daily basis by many, but in themselves are difficult to talk about openly. This in turn leads to secret thoughts and feelings remaining hidden.

The image on the cover of this book illustrates that sometimes secrets are staring us in the face. You will see the word Secret sitting behind the title implying that aspects of secrets are always visible.

Don't knock the gas man from 'Passages' is included in this collection alongside its sister poem which was written at the same time

This anthology features a poem from teenage poet Jewel Nyamekeyi Ewers.

Contents

The Secret

The secret

For better for worse
In sickness and in health
I said these words with delight
Bursting with excitement

Overflowing joy
Heavily scented bouquets
Crisp celebratory champagne
All conspired to make the day memorable
I was living my dream
Two families forever united
Finally I was married to you

The dream rapidly
Spiralled downwards
Into a nightmare

It's been 13 years

We live within our secret
Hidden from the world
You suffer from a mental illness
What was once quirky

I now recognise as symptoms
Leading us to late nights in A&E
Seeking an admission
To aid your recovery

The secret is well masked
Excuses and lies
Have enabled us both
To function well at work
But cracks are appearing elsewhere
Our beautiful children
Are now asking me about
Your odd behaviour
I'm at a loss as to what to say

I'm torn to shreds inside
I've given multiple apologies
With no real explanation
As to why we can't
Attend family functions
I now do anything
To avoid the eyes
Of my mother and sisters
Who if they knew
Would be devastated

The family name would
Be ruined forever

In my culture
Mental illness leads to
Social isolation
My family
Would be treated as
An underclass
To be avoided
Just in case
We contaminate
Their world, their existence

I look at wedding pictures
Hardly recognising myself
A vivacious confident happy woman
Now diminished
Almost extinct

It is ironic
I have worked so hard
To keep our secret
That I am now in fact
Socially isolated

Unsupported
No one to talk to
Desperately unhappy
Living in the shadows
Trapped by my vows

A vacuum

You have been
The background landscape of my life
A burning sun sitting
On the clearly defined blue grey horizon
The perfect picture
Now smashed to smithereens

I am haunted by recurring visions of
Your still lifeless form
Not responding
To my shaking, shouting or wailing
My mind plays, rewinds
And plays the scene
Over and over

Daily I struggle with the pain
Unsure of how to make it go away
No one understands, not friend, or family
I don't even want them to mention you

I'm under pressure to act normal
Whatever that is
At school and at home

I don't get it
How can there ever be normal
Without you?

Unseen silent tears dampen my pillow
When I am alone
I feel that when you crossed
From life to death
You took a huge chunk of me

People want me to look ahead
Exams, college and careers
Why are they so blind?
I can't see past your departure
You had plans
Where are they now?
Just wasted effort and ideas

Even in the middle of a happy crowd
I feel lonely without you
I am left aching for your
Friendship
Hugs and love
I miss you Dad

Abandoned

Every day you spend ages
Looking at me
Your reliable mirror
Sometimes more than twice a day

You critique your face
Trying to spy any further signs of aging
Checking out
If the new anti-wrinkle cream
Is really working

You deftly spot the emerging grey hairs
Which spark a debate in your mind
About whether and when
To dye your thinning curls
Black, blue-black or maroon-black
Or even blonde
Options for masking the inevitable

I note you never look further down
Than your crinkled neck
Your breasts
Are no longer important to you

As far as you are concerned
They are past their used by date
Their source of sexual pleasure
Now on intervals
Significantly reduced in frequency
Months of feeding
Are a far away memory
Children now approaching
Mid-life crises of their own

But if you pay attention
I will show you signs
That things may be amiss
With the health of your breasts
A lump or thickened tissue
Dimpling on the skin
A change in the size or shape
A discharge from your nipples
A rash on or around them
A change in the appearance
Of your nipple
Or even a lump or swelling
In your armpits

In truth
You have abandoned
Your breasts
But the loss of your interest
Could lead to the death of you

At the end of the day

As the russet sun
Waves goodbye to the day
The sultry sound of mellow ripples
Delicately dance on the coastline
Intoxicated, I was drawn
To the rocky shore
With careful steps
I approached the sea
Desperate for cool waves
To caress my feet

As I stood in the water
Watching the soft purple cotton clouds
Travel across the sky
I was no longer alone
Serenity and joy
Became my companions
We conversed and exchanged ideas
In a sphere where time had no dominion

Just as the sun departed
It snatched the moment
Reality struck me in the face

Jolting my thoughts
To the day's events

Confused and nervous
I made my way
Reluctantly back home

The little girl left in the room

As we travelled through life
Hand in hand
Comforted by the other's presence
Death came and squeezed you
From my grip
Leaving me desperately alone
In the room

I regress from an adult
To a little girl
Left
Waiting for her Daddy to come back
Tears spring from within
As I wait

Feelings re-emerging
From past moments
Spent sitting on the bottom step
In the passage
Anticipating your return from work
Knowing I'll recognise
The sound of your car
Despite so many passing our door

My waiting always rewarded by
Your loving smile

Confronted by the truth
Her Daddy is not returning
This little girl faces an endless wait
No more warm smiles
Laughter or dancing

Waves of abandonment
Overtake me
As I struggle not to drown
A wail from the centre of my soul
Rips through the silent room
As I wait.

Broken

Broken
No longer accepted
Often overlooked in preference of another
Rejected and full of grief

I remember once being whole
With endless opportunities
And possibilities ahead of me
I was proud of who I was
Confident in my ability
To execute any task
I loved being the first choice

Suddenly, life circumstances
Snapped my spirit
Leaving me broken
Confidence destroyed by
Fear, doubt and neglect

Now I've slipped into the background
Watching others shine
Relegated to the last choice

A friend followed me into
My dark shadows
And prayed for me
This friend reminded me
There are still endless opportunities
And possibilities ahead of me
The essence of me has not changed

My friend went on to say
He is the One who can
Restore me
To my original beauty, if I let Him
To Him my life is immensely valuable
With a unique purpose
With Him, I can create a work of art

Now I say, I was once broken

Fondled but not cherished

At first glance, it would appear that
We are the favourite part of your body
We are reassured
By your brief but frequent
Unconscious fondling
Throughout the day
You never fail to disregard
Social graces to ensure
We do not suffer an itch
You are careful to ensure we are placed
Correctly within our garment
Any time, any place

You laugh
But explain why
You don't give us any close scrutiny
Ensuring we are ok
If we were your partner's breasts
You would detect changes
In an instant

Why not treat us the same?
Do you have the balls to tell your GP

About the sharp pain in your scrotum?
Take proper care of us please
We want to have a long
And productive life
Not one cut off in its prime

Humiliation

It started with what I thought were
Playful slaps on the arm
Whenever I seemed
To get something wrong
Or you felt I had been stupid
In some way
When I jokingly told you they hurt
You told me not to be a sissy
The blood filled patches on my skin
Were no deterrent for you

You think I don't know
That you hacked
Into my emails
And social media accounts
Telling lies to people behind my back
I have tried so hard to deal
With your constant insecurity

One summer's day
Your slaps turned into pinches
Leaving their burn marks on my skin
I started wearing long sleeve shirts

As I didn't want people
To think I was self-harming
I secretly hoped the thin cloth would
Protect me in some way from the
Fiery sting

Knuckle filled punches
Soon made their way
To my back, chest and arms
Often I'd lay in bed
Unable to move
My flesh throbbing
Soreness determining my stillness
Now I involuntarily flinch
At your touch

I never live up to your expectations
Always deficient in some way
In what I say and what I do
Humiliation stops me
Disclosing my anguish
To anyone

My male friends
Will taunt me about

Being beaten up by a mere woman
My family will curse me for
Not taking charge in my own home

My mind is fragmented
Not knowing what to do
I can't hit back
That would make me just as bad
I can't disclose it to my GP
As my children will be taken away
Through some safeguarding process
Leaving their lives ruined by
The social care system
All because
I couldn't bear a bit of discomfort

Money is a way out
But I don't have enough
To set up my own home with my children
Joint assets tie me to a woman
I no longer love or
Trust to be alone with our children

I feel worthless

Love?

Love has drained away
From its plastic mould
I purposefully move away
From your caress
Paradoxically gentle
With a rough rugged surface
Your wet kiss
Catapults me to a sensation similar
To me lying in an ants' nest
Invisible feet
Scurrying across my body
I struggle to contain my silent scream
Daily you seek to display your affection
I can't bear it

There are times when
Selfishly I use you to satisfy
A transient need
This is always followed
By self-hatred
For a display of weakness

This rapidly turns to indignation
I have a right to take
What I want
When I want it
Regardless of your feelings
After all I've earned it
Simply by staying with you

I am simultaneously
Frustrated and amazed
At your ability to remain content
In my presence
Despite my persistent cold shoulder

Ultimately I am sorry I can no longer
Give you the love you deserve
But I do appreciate your company

My husband the sex offender

Two Christian young people
I thought our marriage was truly
A match made in heaven
But now I've discovered that it was
A complete sham
You have spent our entire marriage
Sleeping with under-age girls
Children

Every day I wake up
I put shame on like a coat
I cry in the bath
Because I never feel clean
I wonder if you ever thought of me
During our times of passion
Or if you had other images
In your mind

I don't know how to tell our children
That you'll never be coming home

You have marred my Christian walk
Now my prayers are limited
To a few words

I hate you
I hope they tear up your backside
In prison
So you can feel a small portion
Of the agony I'm feeling

There are days I wish
I could kill you
Slowly and painfully

You have mutilated the lives of so many
Forced girls to live
Daily with feelings of guilt
Low self-esteem
Together we are your victims

Now I can only pray
"Lord heal us"

My delight

I admire your desire
To make others laugh
Bringing happiness and joy
Into their lives
Your hugs convey
Your openness to love
Completely
No holding back

You are so handsome my Son
Your smooth cinnamon skin
Mahogany almond shaped eyes
Reflecting your inner strength
Lips the colour of a rosy coral
Ready to beam at a moment's notice

Thinking back
Your first smile
Lit a candle in my heart
And every smile since has
Kept that warm glow
Flowing through me

I delight in your ability
To think of alternative
Solutions to problems
You have the qualities
Of a great leader
I can't wait to see
You arrive at your
Full potential

I'm so glad you are
My Son

Not really mine

After 45 years of calling you mine
I now realise that you weren't for keeps
With one extended breath you left me
Not because you wanted to go
But because you couldn't stay
Behind remains your love
Which will last until
I exhale my own final breath

Regret

While others leave beaming
Clutching their womb filled scans
Excited at the growth of life they depict
I leave in emotional turmoil
From a whirlwind of
Guilt and sorrow
The scan I shoved into my bag
Showed an emptied womb

For days I dreamt of the relief
This moment would bring
Believing that my life would
Return to normal
Just because my body was no longer shared

I've discovered that
Normal is gone
I forever hold the secret memory of you
The child I could not
Bear to love or
Bear to bare

I really believed that
An ended life
Was better than the one
You would have had with me
This thought circled around my mind
For days like vultures around
A dying carcass

There are days when I wonder
What our life together
Would have been like
Whether your hair would be
Straight or curly
Your eyes blue or brown
Whether you would have been
A happy or melancholy child

I have pushed the torment
Of not having you
So deep inside
That most of the time
I just feel numb
But I am cognisant
Of the fact
That I am rotting inside

As there are episodes
When the hurt
Emerges as a toxic vapour of rage
Particularly when I am asked
Why I have not got any children

I planned to have a family
When the conditions were right
But when I was ready
Conception evaded me

Now my child bearing years are over
I am filled with deep regret
You were my only chance

Now I face life knowing
I'll never be the Mum
I wanted to be

Selfish

Suddenly
My body stopped working as it should
I am ill, seriously ill
Moment by moment
Mortality strikes me in the face
Reminding me that my days are numbered

You prattle on trying to bring normality
To an abnormal situation
Constantly tidying an immaculate home
Unsolicited offers of food and drink
Are trying my nerves

I prefer solitude
It is a space
Where I can consider my dreams
With the understanding
That they will remain unmet

Attending my children's weddings
Teaching and playing with grandchildren
A hot air balloon ride
Countries I had planned to visit

Food I had longed to taste
All slipping from my grasp

As I travel around
I notice the amazing aspects of nature
But sadness overwhelms me
When I see dying flowers
Sun burnt grass
And lifeless animals

You speak of me locking you out
By not discussing my illness
Showing a total lack of insight
Into my plight
Talking to you means
That I have to cope
With your anxieties
Uncertainty and tears
All of which just saps me
Of what little energy I have

Yes I am selfish
If I can't live for me now
Do as I please for once
When will I get another opportunity?

Wrapped up in myself

This illness
Which eats away at your body
Is also consuming our relationship
Shared laughter and fun
Has been replaced by
Silence
Lack of intimacy
Sadness and depression

I am desperate for us
To use the time we have left
To create pleasurable lasting
Memories for me
I want so much to live
Like we used to
In and out of each-others pockets
Every thought shared
I want the memory of
Your smile and laughter
Seared on my heart in these last days
I feel dismissed and neglected
My best friend disappeared
With one sentence from a doctor

When I am away from you
I consider our dreams
Attending our children's weddings
Teaching and playing
With our grandchildren
Countries we had planned to visit
Food we had longed to taste
All of which will be buried with you

Nothing is normal
I live in a dimension of uncertainty
I don't know how to act around you
I talk about everyday stuff
In an attempt to reach out to you
Rebuffed by your silence
I feel stupid for speaking
About trivial things
I mask my true feelings
When I am with you
I know I can't make you feel better
But I am trying my best
I feel helpless
As I watch your daily decline

Each sunrise
Sucks more energy from you
Popping to the toilet
Has become a shuffle
To the commode
With accidents on the way
I am now resigned
To our present existence
Happy to show my love
By keeping you clean
Holding your hand whilst
You unseeingly watch the TV
Sitting in silence for hours on end
I have become accepting of the morsel
You consume before declaring
You are full
No longer forcing you to eat more

I now realise that the only gift
I can give to you is
Allowing our relationship
To end on your terms

Tête-à-tête

I

As I approach you
The curtains on
The windows of your eyes draw shut
Outwardly you smile
Giving a warm greeting with an
Outstretched hand
Whilst your internal body stance
Reminds me of an athlete
On the starting line of a race
As I confront you
Probing why you're running away
Embarrassed laughter lingers in the air
You swiftly deny
Not wanting to be in my presence
Sadly what I have experienced with you
Is a familiar ritual I am party to
With various people
Throughout each day
Maybe I should change my approach

II

I must be quick....too late
The jail door slams
I'm locked into a pointless conversation
With no means of escape
I try to be nice, but need to get away
You sense my desperate desire
For an immediate exit
I cringe under the spotlight
Smiling through the horror of exposure
I try to repair the damage
But it's too late

The chocolate cake

Equipped with
My apron and electric mixer
I excitedly set of on my journey of
Making a rich moist chocolate cake
I had carefully studied the
Recipe and tantalising image
In my cookbook for weeks
Salivating at the thought
Of the first delicious bite

I gleefully begin
By mixing the sugar and butter
As per the instructions
In my trusted book
As my confidence grew
I saw no reason not to be a little creative
A little vanilla perhaps accompanied by
A teaspoon of chilli
That's the new thing
Chilli chocolate

As I spoon the mixture into the cake tin
I decide I want to have

A melting chocolate centre
Oozing out of my cake
So I add a little chocolate frosting
To the middle of the mixture

As I wait for the cake to be ready
I frequently look at my watch.
Whilst whipping double cream
Into soft peaks
And hulling strawberries
To imitate the picture
In my book

At last the time has come
I test the cake
A clean knife emerges
From my work of genius
I carefully remove
The cake from the oven
So as not to drop the tin

I can't adequately describe my shock
At what happened next.....

My cake EXPLODED!!!!
Frosting and lumps of cake
Found its way
Into every crevice of my oven
Kitchen cupboard doors and floor
My once white apron
Face and hair
Was splattered
With a mingled mass of brown
Sponge filled sauce

I sat dejected on the floor
Staring with disbelief
At what remained of my dream

The painting

I am a painting that has been
Consigned to the corners of the attic
By its owner

Layers of grime now hide
My once vibrant pigments
Which now lack lustre and
Are indecipherable

The only life around me
Is evidenced by
The delicately spun webs of spiders
And flashes of brown-black creatures
Which create illusion and confusion
For the mind
I am alone and forgotten

One day the owner remembers me
I am grabbed and hauled
To the One who restores

The restorer handles me with
Gentleness and wonder

Appreciating my value
He carefully dabs away
Each layer of filth
Acquired over the years
Anger, despair, heartbreak
Abuse, neglect and shame

As he works
One by one
Colours, tints and shades appear
The image begins to emerge
Pulsating with life

The assignment is finished
The owner then recognises
That the painting
Her inner self
Is a masterpiece

Vanished

My heart breaks into shards
Like ice under a pick
At your words reflecting limitless love
You wonder why I cry
Face turned elsewhere
The truth is
I'm terrified
Of not being the me
You want me to be
Strong, courageous
And triumphant

In my reality
The true me is a hazy mist
Intangible to my touch
Always just out of my grasp
I've struggled for
Hours, days, weeks and years
Now, it's just too much effort

I can't even pretend
Present a fake image
As when reflected in your love

I am consumed by
Inadequacy
And self-contempt

Even though I know
You would try to understand
If I explained my hellish existence
The facts will drag you into my
Desolate, manic,
Disordered, subsistence
A one way trip with no way of returning
To your pure, innocent,
Ordered, heavenly, universe

I really do love you
The best way I can show you
Is to just to leave
Without a word

Don't' knock the gas man

I'm telling you girlfriend
The Gas Man is coming TODAY!
I can't wait

As soon as I got the Gas appointment
I sorted out the others
Hair, Nails, Facial
I selected my outfit
With such precision
And attention to detail
I'm dressing to entice
Seduction in mind
The Gas Man is coming TODAY

Who says you have to get out there
To find an attractive man
He's coming right into my home
Let me tell you
This Gas Man
Can inspect my pipe any time
He's so fine
You see he's been before
Tall, lean, and strong

I caught myself drooling
At his taught frame the last time
Oh the Gas Man is coming TODAY
I can't wait

I open the door playing it cool
He and his mate enter
With trivial conversation
I calmly offer tea
Trying to hide the fact that
My heart is racing
My pupils are dilating
Goodness, my mouth is so dry

I agree with him that he should come
And check out the pipes in my bedroom
Whilst his mate works downstairs

Well, sister don't knock the Gas Man
He knows his stuff
How to give a good service
You know what I mean
Mmmmm
Did the Gas Man come today you ask?
Yep, he sure did

The gas man ????

The Gas Man is coming today is he?
Why is this so significant?

Yes I heard you
But why Sis
What deep seated need
Can he really meet?
He's literally just passing through
A fleeting fancy
Nothing permanent

I ask myself
If your moans of pleasure
Were really the sounds of pain?
Reflecting your unmet desire
To be loved for who you actually are

I know you desperately wish to have
A stable fulfilling relationship
With a man of your own
I see it in your eyes

You are beautiful
Full of vibrancy
With an attractive personality

There no need for you
To let the Gas man knock you

Just sit back
Relax
Love will seek you out

The marvellous handbag

As I sit at my desk lamenting
With my pals
Spitefulness and envy
A plan of deceit flourishes in my mind
I wring a few tears from
The dry reservoir of my soul
Nursing the hope that
My boss will allow me
To leave work early
I'm dying to rush out to the shops
To purchase the amazing handbag
I saw my friend Jane
Modelling at the weekend

My spiralling journey
Into the whirlpool of jealousy
Was halted by panic
My overly tactile colleague
Was glancing my way
At best her appearance
Can be described as "lived in"
At worst she looked like she's been
Around the block more times

Than anyone could possibly count
Eyes brimming with sympathy
She advances
Her rose scented massive bosom
Threatening to smother my face
Cutting off my air
In her hugging action
I deftly move
With the agility of a rugby player
Avoiding the crushing huddle of bodies

Her aim is to console
But I detest being touched
Especially by her
She often barges
Uninvited into my personal space
But it's cruel to shun her
So I spin a tale of sorrow and despair
Whilst keeping a safe space between us

I gratefully accept her offer
To tell the boss I had to leave
Masking my glee
Whilst picturing my new bag

Tears

As your warm tear drops
Roll down my skin
A conversation begins
Your tears tell me about
Your inability to influence
A desperately worrying situation
They speak of your helplessness
Whilst trying to be strong for others

My heart melts like a candle
Under the flame of your anguish

I pray asking God to intervene
To bring about a good conclusion
Whilst I embrace you
In the hope of giving
Some sort of consolation

The F word

So my brother
You want to have your helmet tickled
You have come to church
Given your offering
And now you're looking for
Any sister who will oblige

You justify your pleasure
By convincing yourself
That lack of penetration
Means your not engaging in the "F" word
It's all so easy
One text, one Call
Leads to total satisfaction
A complete release

But my brother
Are you prepared
To stand before your maker and
Argue that Fellatio is not Fornication?
Whatever the 'F' word
In His eyes it is sin

Voice of passion

Can you hear the voice of passion?
Or have you pressed
Your internal mute button
As you're not interested in the words
You don't want to
Surf on sound waves to places
Such as uncertainty
Vulnerability and scrutiny

Can you hear the voice of passion?
Or are you suffering
From cardiac deafness?
A soundless world of inactivity
Watching life pass by
Afraid to do something, anything
Paralysed

Can you hear the voice of passion?
Speaking words of
Direction and purpose
Listen there's a message just for you
That voice of passion
Gives life

What is the point?

What's the point of living
When I have no hope?

I plead with family for help
But love and compassion are
Concealed by the
Shroud of unforgiveness

Past words spat out coated by loathing
Have tasered friends to the ground
Where I have stepped over them
Leaving them behind unattended
My rage sparking the words
'I don't need you'

Reflecting I see
I never had time
For overly friendly neighbours
And their invitations to socialise
My terse words ensured
They never spoke to me again

Now I sit alone
With the noose of loneliness
Around my neck

I have no one to call
To see if I am ok
To tell me that
I am loved and valued

The coarse truth is
I don't believe
I am loveable anymore
I despise who I have become

Although I am physically alive
I am dead inside
Withered and decomposed
Facing no future

I may as well
Bring it all to a close

Hope

There is hope
In the outstretched arms of Jesus
A place of refuge
Where unconditional love
Is waiting to surround you
Lifting you up from despair
He doesn't see your flaws
He doesn't judge
He receives you as you are
No criticism, no rejection
He is the embodiment
Of forgiveness and acceptance

He is the friend
Who is ever present
To wipe your tears
And whisper words of comfort
To your heart

He died just so that
He could care for you
Ensuring a secure future
Filled with the promises
Of God our Father

To listen, to provide
To protect, to heal

Once you have decided to
Walk with Him as your
Lord and Saviour
You will realise that
He has always been there
To catch you when you fall
You will make mistakes
But if you allow Him
He will guide you through them
To a place of peace and renewal

The choice

I see you

I desire you

But I can't choose

I contemplate

On the fact

That the choice

Is not mine

But yours

Sundown

As companions
We had a special understanding
It was enough to be in the same room
No interaction necessary
Other than to express an unmet need

You reminded me of
A sunset kissing the midnight sky
A delightful melody
Of oranges, browns, yellows
Whites and black
Played each time you moved
Yes, you were amazingly beautiful

Your health declined
I became desperately sad
As you refused food and water
Your life once vibrant
Wafted away like a mist
You reached out to me
For one last touch

I held you
Hoping with the right treatment
You would recover in a few days

I get a call
A soft compassionate voice
Explains you will not be alive
At the end of the day
Politeness demands I say thank you
For the devastating news

I couldn't be with you
As you fell asleep
Time did not permit

Now I smile
At your favourite spot in the room
Taking comfort in the fact
That you knew you were loved

My garden

Along an amazing alley are
Beautiful, bold black blooms,
Colourful carnations, corsage cattleya
Dancing daffodils, delightful daisies
Entertaining eagerly experienced eyes
Footloose foxgloves freely flick freesias
Golden germini gather gracefully
Honeysuckle happily hugging hyacinths
Instantly inspiring innovation
Justifiably joyful
Kennedia kiss
Lovingly, lazily languishing
My mind muses, meditating
Noting numerous
Omnifarious, obliviously
Pleasing perennial posies
Quietly quenching questioning
Readily rendering replenishment
Sweet smelling scents swelling
Tones, tints, traveling towards
Us, ultimately unhindered

Vibrant variegation, vapour void
Wasps wafting willfully
Xenic,
Yearning, yawning
Zeal, zapped.....zzzzz

The seasons

Summer notes
Dancing on the soles
Of my feet

As Autumn leaves
Snow-flakes float towards
The waiting ground

Winter tears
Run down my withered
Worn face

Sprouting Spring
A cacophony of colours assault
My ears and eyes

Seeds

I have given you a handful of seeds
Please take the time
To value what I have
Entrusted you with
Visualise the harvest
I have planned for you

Seek out good ground
Be quick to discard
Unsuitable conditions
For my seeds
Then sow

Tend with love
The suckling gifts and talents
Ideas and passions
I have placed within your care
Feed and water them
Grant them shade when required

Let patience be your guide
Protect your potential harvest
From parasites who come

To gnaw away at
Your will to see things through
Whether they be negative people
Self-doubt or discouragement

Diligence, assertiveness and faith
Will ensure you will reap
The bountiful harvest I have for you
Not only that
But you will impact the lives
I predestined for you
To touch
Leaving me saying
I am well pleased

Mummy

Mummy
Beautiful in the sight of everyone
Her meticulous presentation
Was evidence of her exquisite taste
I am proud she was My Mummy

Family and friends
Relied on her sound advice
Concerning everything
Often they would not
Purchase a piece of clothing or furniture
Without her by their side

Some called her proud
Others called her feisty
She was straightforward
She would speak her mind
Leaving you in no doubt
About where you stood
But we all knew she was also
Very thoughtful and kind

Family was always central to her life
I remember my childhood exciting
Luxurious summer holidays
Where Cutex and the pressing comb
Transformed my rural look
Into the sophisticated image of town
I have fun-filled memories
Etched on my mind
Of trips to the hustle and bright lights
Of town on Saturday evenings by bicycle
With me precariously placed
On the handle bars
The two of us
Spending precious time together

Cold Britain saw Mummy arrive in 1965
Along with Daddy they faced the challenges
Of establishing a life for me to move into
When I arrived a little while later
Living in one room
Heated by a paraffin heater
Sharing a kitchen and bathroom
Was the standard amongst
Friends and relatives
So different to our lives in Jamaica

I smile when I think
About Mummy picking the fluff
From our candlewick spread
Out of my hair
That stuff seemed to get everywhere

I chuckle when I remember that
Mummy never skimped on money
Ensuring that I got the best
She spared no expense

My parents did not joke with my upbringing
I was raised in a strict household
They wanted to protect me from so much
An opportunity for nurse training
And life in the nursing home
Became my youthful escape to freedom

Mummy loved life
She was tenacious
She got on with things
Never the victim
Always the conqueror

I reminisce on the times
My children and I went on holiday
Always returning to a fridge she had
Jam-packed with food during our absence
She constantly took care of us

As she got older
Dementia slowly
Tucked parts of Mummy away
Into a secret place
Starting with her memory
Eventually stealing her ability to walk
Care for and feed herself
It was tough to watch
She hated being so reliant on others
And resisted assistance for a while
As this went against all
She had stood for in life
Her pride was the one thing
Dementia struggled to
Snatch away from her
As I painfully witnessed these changes
I found refuge in the fact
That she always knew
She was loved and well cared for

Eventually Mummy closed her eyes
One last time

A huge void has been left behind
That nothing or no one can fill
Although I have been supported
By family, friends and brethren
I still face many lonely times
When I am left
To ponder thoughts and memories
Leading to silent tears
Escaping from my soul

I miss you Mummy
I will never get over losing you
I will just learn to manage life
Without you a little better
Day by day

Betrayal

Growing up
My Dad was the centre of my world
He always read me bedtime stories
He willing played the endless games
I made up

Not that I didn't love my Mum
She is an amazing woman
But she shared her special times
With my brother

As I got older
Dad helped me with my homework
Took me to museums and art galleries
Concerts and parks
He always wanted me
To have the best

I vowed that when I got older
I would marry a man
Exactly like my Dad
My hero

Today I came home early from school
I called out for my Dad
Because I knew he was not at work
I went to my parent's room
As I thought he was sleeping
I really wanted to tell him
About school today

When I walked in
He wasn't there
But the shiny flash of a condom packet
Caught my eye
It lay opened on his bedside table
At first I was confused
Because Mum is on holiday
Then I detected the hint of
An unfamiliar perfume in the room

As horror crept through my body
Revulsion started to wring
The contents of my stomach
I rushed to the bathroom
My head spinning
A migraine emerging

As I stood at the sink
Rinsing my mouth I spotted
A long strand of hair on the tap
Brunette in colour
Definitely from a different gene pool
We are of African decent
Short and curly
Are the hallmarks of our hair

I felt sick again
But there was nothing left in my stomach
Tears burned a pathway down my cheeks
As I tried to fathom
How Dad could betray me
My perfect image of him
Destroyed

My identity changed in a moment
I am now the child of an adulterer

Rage begins to pulsate
With every heartbeat
As I recall the recent
Whispered phone calls
Absent mindedness

Forgotten arrangements
To do things together
My time with him
Has been sacrificed
So that he could spend
Time with HER

My poor Mum
She has loved him
For more than 20 years
I have silently admired her
As she both pampered
And supported my Dad
With his endeavours

What I am I going to do?
I don't know how
To form the words
That I know will break her heart
How do I confront my Dad?
I don't even think
I can bear to speak to him
I hear a key in the door
Oh God
Help me!

Idiot

I have just come home
My sister is gushing stuff
About Dad having an affair

Stupid idiot
I thought I would have time
To clean up the place
Remove the evidence
Of my secret sin
If I had just stopped to
Check if I left anything behind

It's been two months since
I've been sneaking her in
I didn't take her to my room
'Cos I thought she might think
It looks childish
With my posters
And single bed
I've got some things
I have treasured for years
I didn't want her to mock me

By taking pictures
And sharing on Snapchat

I felt so grown up
In my parent's room
As I lay there
I imagined
What it would be like
To have a wife and
Home of my own

My sister is so wounded
I have never seen her
This low
I guess I'll have to own up
And put her out of her misery

Oh man
Now she's sobbing
Out of control
I can't make her stop
She feels mortified
About thinking Dad was guilty

Maybe I should have kept my mouth shut

Blue funk

I sit here realising that
So many men think
They want what I have
Wonderful kids
Fantastic wife
Beautiful home
Successful job

But depression gnaws
Holes in my soul
Like a mouse
Chewing it's way
Through paper

My world
My mind
Is crumbling

Depression has convinced me
That I have no worth
To anyone
If I died today
It would be a relief for everyone

I have never felt truly loved
Because as a child my Mother left me
With smiles and a promise
It would not be for long
That it was for the best

I spent seven years
Asking myself
Why did she leave me behind?
She was absent whilst
I journeyed from a boy
To a young man
I concluded
She thought her life was better off
Without me

If she needed me
Like I needed her
She would have returned
To rescue me
From care givers
Who didn't care
I was fed and educated
But there was no evidence
That I was loved or even wanted

Now I recognise that Miss Daphne
Couldn't do anything differently
Because of her own stunted growth
She just replicated life as she knew it

Reunited at last
With a stranger
Called Mother
A purely functional name
With no emotional attachment

When I witnessed that her life
Had moved on without me
I was filled with animosity
I was expected to be pleasant
To new siblings
Who were so unlike me
In both speech and attitude
The only common denominator
Being a shared mother

They never actually
Understood or accepted me
I was just too different
I made my mind up then

That I would show them all
I supressed my bitterness
Pushing it into the
Dark crevices of my soul
I worked hard
To create my ideal of a family
A life I defined
As successful
I stood on the pinnacle of pride

When my Mother passed away
Shortly after my 50th birthday
It unleashed unprecedented
Periods of desperately low moods
I felt that all I had carefully
Designed and built around me
No longer mattered

There have been times
When I have sat listening
To the hustle and bustle of my family
Just wanting to disappear
Whispered conversations with
The Samaritans
Hasn't stopped me feeling that there

Is nothing of value left of me
I am dreadfully alone
I don't know what to do
Oh God
Help me!

The pain of leaving

As I stood before you
Trying to put on my bravest face
Speaking words of reassurance
My heart was breaking into a million pieces
It won't be long I said
Not really knowing
How long it would be
Until I saw you again
The sight of your immense
Sadness pierced me
At the very centre
My head immediately
Began to feel as if
My eyes were being squeezed
Out of my head
So much pressure

One last hug
One last kiss

As I turned around
Tears ran down my face
I battled against my body's desire to

Scream out and run back to you
I just had to keep walking forward
For our future's sake

Over the next two weeks
I could not control the sobs
As they escaped
At their own will
Friends tried to console me
But their words could not fill
The void created
By being separated from you, son

The excitement
That should have been present
At travelling to a new land
Experiencing new places, food and people
Were non-existent
I felt as if I was walking in a grey cloud
Barely aware of the things around me

I was missing you so much
Your smile, your touch, your laugh
I could no longer cook with you
Attend to your clothes

Watch you while you sleep
I had to depend
On someone else
To do this
Knowing all the time
There was no way
They could do it as well as I could

Daily, I hoped you didn't
Forget how much I loved you
I tried to write letters to remind you
Sending what I could
There were days
When I sat and wondered
How much had you grown?
What would you tell me
If you had the chance?
How did you get on at school that day?
Were you behaving yourself?

I learnt to live
With the dull ache of loss
Marked by frequent
Bursts of depression

Seven years have passed
A day has not gone by
Without me thinking about you
Wondering if I made the right decision
Seven years of scrimping and saving
Denying myself, sticking to the basics
So that you could eventually join me

I am at the airport
Finally, we are to be together again
I can't wait for us to share a joke
Just like we used to

I am so excited
My palms are sweaty
I can't keep still
As I sit down
I immediately stand up
Unable to resist the urge
To keep moving
I can see people coming out
Who were on your flight
There are tell tale
Signs of bronzed arms
Carrying duty free boxes of rum

Oh God of grace
I see a young man
Who has your eyes
Your complexion
Your walk

I call out your name
The young man responds
I rush to him and hug him
He is stiff in my arms
He greets me formally
Very polite in his manner
I notice the flicker
Of anger in his eyes

It dawns on me
My little boy is gone
Nowhere to be found
I have been reunited
With a stranger
Bearing my son's name

The holiday

As I lie here
Sunrays delicately
Stroke away the tension
Resident in my body
As I meditate
I struggle to identify
The last time
I was so relaxed

This holiday is my planned escape
From family, friends and work
Or should I say
Duty, obligation and necessity

I am free
I can do what I want
Go where I want
Eat what I want
Without the burden
Of someone else's view
I wish I could live like this
All the time

Responsibility has me bound
Like a slave
My identity, desires and liberty
Stripped away over the years
Always someone's
Wife, mother, daughter, co-worker
Previous attempts to exercise my choice
Has led to recriminations and
Failure to meet "their" expectations

If the truth be told
I am angry and resentful
Constantly grieving the loss
Of my dreams.....

The career I didn't quite have
The countries I didn't get to explore
Even the art classes I relinquished
Because my family thought
It was a silly idea of mine
Right now I just want walk away
From my husband and children
Towards a new start
Basking in the rays of the sun

My divine gift

Just the perfect gift

Each dawn births something new

Watching you mature sparks a

Euphoric mix of pleasure and pride with

Love and laughter shared perpetually

Loving you to death

The door slammed shut
As your spirit left the room
I stood clutching the pillow
I had used to end
Our entwined lives
Dementia had been stealing
You away from me rapidly
I fought back
The only way I knew how
Filled with a sense of triumph
I stand facing loneliness
Still in love with you

The paper crown

I entered the coffee shop
For our habitual afternoon meet up
My usual latte is in position
Waiting for me
I later realise
This was your attempt
To purchase absolution

A few words spoken
Left me shrouded in
The mantle of rejection
Feeling unlovable
Feeling untouchable
Like faeces dumped in the street
The hot steam of yesterday's love
Disappearing in a vapour

Dumped
No longer desirable in your eyes
Anger engulfs me

A few weeks on
I stand wearing my
Army camouflage uniform
The green of envy intertwined
With the brown of rejection
I fight a daily battle with
Loneliness and despondency
My mind has been overpowered
By them so many times

In war there are
No boundaries, No rules
One day the blood of betrayal
Seeps into my clothing
Following my vicious attack
My friendship of 30 years
Is slaughtered
As I strike up an intimate relationship
With her husband

She didn't want him anymore
Twenty years of marriage
Ended six months ago
So what if I was their
Chief bridesmaid

This is war
Each woman for herself
I now sit revelling in my conquest
I imagine myself
Wearing a jewel encrusted crown
Filled with emeralds, rubies
Sapphires and diamonds
Finally, I am desirable and wanted

I am oblivious to the fact that
Others see me
As a naked woman
Wearing just a paper crown
A childlike construction
Coloured in with crayon
Exposing the tattoos on each breast
Low self-esteem and
Low self-worth

Diamond trapped in stone

By

Jewel Nyamekeyi Ewers

Diamond trapped in stone

So many times
I've wondered
What it would take
What I would have to do
To get you
To realise your potential
And get you to think
Why someone else's criticism
Should be influential
And cause corruption
Towards your decision
To spread your wings
And fly with your belief
You see
Cause they're thieves
Stabbing with their claws
Sharp as knives
Stabbing your sides
Your self-confidence and pride
Which before they kept
Hammering on your mind
Forcing you to keep it
Hidden and locked inside

And at that moment
It was all too much
That you
Ignored your self-worth and
Left it behind
Like a dirty bookshelf
Thrown out
Put on the road side
Only difference is
That your self-worth
Was something
You were supposed to be
Carrying for a lifetime
And this effect
It spreads fast
Like a YouTube video
Posted online
Faster than the
Don't judge vines
They still judge
But when you post your story
To get the stress
Off your chest
They hit the dislike button
Calling you an attention seeker

Or think you are lying
But behind the screen
They tap and smudge with their fingers
You're really crying and wanting to die
The pain you tried to expose
The screen is the pain
They didn't want to believe
Or wanted to see
You felt like a rose
Getting trampled
In the ground
Even though
You're still trying to grow
But little did you know
That a rose
That has been trampled
In the ground
Is not destroyed
It may be crippled
But the beauty of it
Is still able to grow
The problems around you
Will soon erode
You will no longer be a
Diamond trapped in stone

Jewel Nyamekeyi Ewers is a young writer who also performs spoken word. Her work has been published in a Teen Poetry anthology and she has performed her poetry at community events including an event at a local Mental Health Trust.

Prayer

There are some issues covered within the poems in this book which may raise painful memories or reflections for the reader.

I have included a prayer below:

Merciful God and Father who through your son Jesus forgives all my sins and makes everything new; You see and know my pain: Thank you for the grace to forgive those who have wronged me and for the strength to cope with the memory of a hurtful past. I decree and declare your word that no weapon formed against me will prosper and that what was meant from evil, is now working for my good. This is a new day and therefore I refuse to hold on to disappointment, bitterness, blame, anger or any negative emotion that has had a foothold in my life. I choose to embrace your promise of a better and brighter future. I choose to live in love and to walk in the pathway of peace. Dear Lord, increase my faith and teach me one step at a time to trust again, to learn from the experience of my past and to make wise decisions concerning the affairs of my life. Help me to understand the purpose for my pain and give me the courage to reach out to others who are going through familiar experiences; So that with the same comfort that you have given to me, I will be able to comfort and strengthen others.

I pray this in Jesus name.

Scripture references: Psalms 103: 3-5; Isaiah 54:17; Genesis 50:20; 2 Corinthians 1:14

Bishop Delroy Powell

National Presiding Bishop of
The New Testament Assembly (England)

Resources

NHS Talking Therapies:
http://www.iapt.nhs.uk/services/

List of low cost counselling services in South
London:
www.caretolisten.co.uk
http://www.southeastlondoncounselling.org.uk
/lowcost.htm;
http://www.itsgoodtotalk.org.uk/ ;

Faith Hope Counselling
The Sanctuary, admin@ntatooting.org.uk
0208 672 9416

Domestic Violence:
http://www.womanstrust.org.uk/;
http://blacknblue.org.uk/pages/dvmyths.php ;
http://www.restoredrelationships.org/resources/

Domestic Violence & Men:
http://www.dvip.org/mens-services.htm /
http://www.respect.uk.net/pages/contact-
us.html

Miscarriage:
http://www.miscarriageassociation.org.uk/

Infertility:
http://www.infertilitynetworkuk.com/

Self-Harm: http://www.harmless.org.uk/

Self Help Resources:
http://www.moodjuice.scot.nhs.uk/
http://www.samaritans.org/

Bereavement: http://www.cruse.org.uk/home /
http://www.wandsworthbereavement.org.uk/

Sexual Abuse:
http://www.aurorahealthfoundation.org.uk/#!links

Rape / Sexual Abuse: (Women)
http://www.rasasc.org.uk/ /
http://www.rapecrisis.org.uk/centres_show.ph
p?area=london

Rape / Sexual abuse: (Men)
http://www.pandys.org/malesurvivors.html

Relationships-
http://www.relate.org.uk/home/index.html.

About the Author

Jacqueline Robinson

Jacqueline has been a Christian from a young age. She is also the author of **Silence is Broken, Passages** and **A voice from behind the veil.** The poems in each of the books have been used to fuel discussions in a number of workshop settings within her local community covering topics such as parenting, bereavement and mental ill health. Jacqueline has been the resident poet at a local Christian women's group for the past six years and has been the guest poet at local library creative writing groups. Jacqueline works alongside community groups to promote the Arts and dialogue.